GREAT SPORTING EVENTS

Rugby

Clive Gifford

W

FRANKLIN WATTS
LONDON • SYDNEY

First published in 2011 by Franklin Watts
338 Euston Road, London NW1 3BH

Franklin Watts Australia
Level 17/207 Kent Street, Sydney NSW 2000

Editors: Katie Dicker and Gerard Cheshire
Art Direction: Rahul Dhiman (Q2AMedia)
Designers: Cheena Yadav, Ravinder Kumar
(Q2AMedia)
Picture researchers: Anubhav Singhal and
Nivisha Sinha (Q2AMedia)

Picture credits:
t=top b=bottom c=centre l=left r=right

Front Cover: Ross Setford/NZPA/AP Photo.
Back Cover: Mark J. Terrill/AP Photo, Aijaz
Rahi/AP Photo, Dave Thompson/AP Photo, Ross
Setford/NZPA/AP Photo, Jay LaPrete/AP Photo,
Anja Niedringhaus/AP Photo.
Title Page: Kamran Jebreili/AP Photo.
Imprint Page: Odd Andersen/AP Photo
Insides: Alastair Grant/AP Photo: 4, Mark Baker/
AP Photo: 5, Francois Mori/AP Photo: 6, Odd
Andersen/AP Photo: 7, Mark Nolan/Getty Images
Sport/Getty Images: 8, Paul Thomas/AP Photo:
9, Tom Hevezi/AP Photo: 10, Claude Paris/AP
Photo: 11, Schalk Van Zuydam/AP Photo: 12,
David Rowland/NZPA/AP Photo: 13, David
Cannon/Getty Images Sport/Getty Images: 14,
Peter Morrison/AP Photo: 15, Richard Lewis/AP
Photo: 16, Will Powers/AP Photo: 17, AP Photo:
18, Themba Hadebe /AP Photo: 19, Vincent Yu/
AP Photo: 20, Kamran Jebreili/AP Photo: 21,
Tertius Pickard/AP Photo: 22, Scott Heppell/AP
Photo: 23, Mike Hewit/Getty Images Sport/Getty
Images: 24, Mark Baker/AP Photo: 25, Dean
Purcell/Getty Images Sport/Getty Images: 26,
Tom Hevezi/AP Photo: 27, AP Photo: 28.

A CIP catalogue record for this book
is available from the British Library.

ISBN: 978 1 4451 0191 0

Dewey Classification: 796.3'33

Note: At the time of going to press, the statistics in this
book were up to date. However, due to the nature of
sport, it is possible that some of these may now be out
of date.

Printed in China

Franklin Watts is a division of Hachette Children's
Books, an Hachette UK company.
www.hachette.co.uk

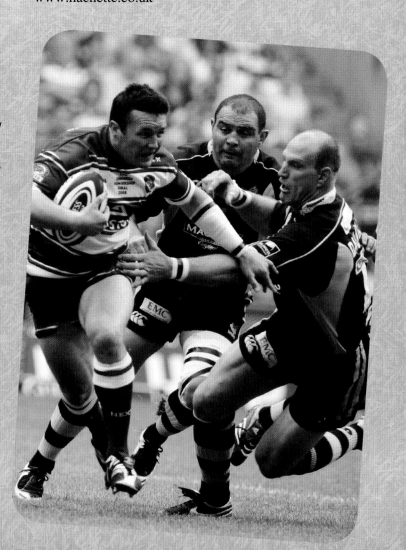

Contents

*Words in **bold** are in the glossary on page 30

Race for the line

Rugby union and rugby league are exciting action sports where teams of players run, pass and kick an oval-shaped ball, beating opponents at high speed to reach the goal line to score a **try**.

Similarities and differences

Both forms of rugby take place on a large grass pitch, with male or female teams competing in a game lasting 80 minutes. There are many differences in rules, however. A rugby union team has 15 players and a rugby league team has 13. There are also no **lineouts** in rugby league.

Tackling defence

The defending team tries to stop the attacking side by **intercepting** passes or tackling the opponent with the ball. In rugby league, a tackled player is allowed to get to his feet and play the ball unopposed. A team gets six tackles before the ball passes to the opposition. In rugby union, there is no set number of tackles and the tackled player must release the ball on the floor once tackled.

Ian Gough, of Wales, goes to catch the ball from a lineout throw during a high-paced rugby union match against Canada.

Scoring points

In both rugby union and rugby league, a try is scored when a player puts the ball down on the in-goal, the area beyond the try line at each end of the pitch. A try is worth five points in rugby union and four in rugby league, and is followed by an attempted **conversion** kick through the goalposts for further points. Players can also score points with a penalty kick. This is awarded to a team when a player on the opposing team has committed a **foul** or broken the rules of the game.

England player Jason Robinson (holding ball) played rugby league for eight years before making the switch to rugby union. Here he is playing in a rugby union match.

Switching sports

Although the rules and **tactics** differ between the two sports, a number of players have switched between them. Two of the most famous were England's Jason Robinson and Australia's Wendell Sailor. Both men were star rugby league players who made the change to rugby union. They played against each other in the 2003 Rugby Union World Cup Final.

GREAT SPORTING STATS

	Rugby league	Rugby union
Number of players	13	15
Points for a try	4	5
Points for a drop goal	1	3
Points for a penalty kick	2	3
Points for a conversion kick	2	2

Club rugby union

Most rugby union clubs compete in a competition based on a league format. Teams play matches at their home grounds and away at their opponent's grounds. They gain points for winning or drawing a game.

Foreign imports

A large number of rugby stars play in leagues far away from their home countries. Argentina's Felipe Contepomi, for example, has played for Bristol in England, Leinster in Ireland and, in 2010, played in France's Top 14 for Toulon, alongside England's Jonny Wilkinson and Scotland's Rory Lamont.

Top 14

France's leading club rugby union competition is also one of the oldest, first held in 1892. Starting in August, the teams play 26 games with the top two teams in the league meeting each other for a grand final, usually held in June. After ten runners-up finishes without ever winning the Top 14, ASM Clermont Auvergne finally triumphed in 2010 beating Perpignan 19-6 in the final.

James Haskell, playing for Stade Français, is tackled by Perpignan's Maxime Mermoz during a Top 14 match.

The Magners League

Previously known as the Celtic League, this competition pits top rugby union sides from Ireland, Wales and Scotland against each other. Fifteen teams began the competition in 2001, but for the 2009/10 season just ten took part – four from Ireland, four from Wales and two from Scotland. Two Italian teams joined the league in the 2010/11 season.

The English Premiership

The English Premiership is the top rugby union league in England and features 12 teams. Since 2000/01, the top four sides at the end of the season contest **semi-finals**, with the winners competing in a single game held at Twickenham Stadium in London for the championship. Leicester Tigers and London Wasps have enjoyed remarkable success in recent years, winning ten of the last 11 titles.

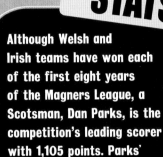

GREAT SPORTING STATS

Although Welsh and Irish teams have won each of the first eight years of the Magners League, a Scotsman, Dan Parks, is the competition's leading scorer with 1,105 points. Parks' points include 18 tries.

London Wasps' Lawrence Dallaglio (right) attempts to tackle Leicester Tigers' Marco Wentzel during the English Premiership final at Twickenham, 2008.

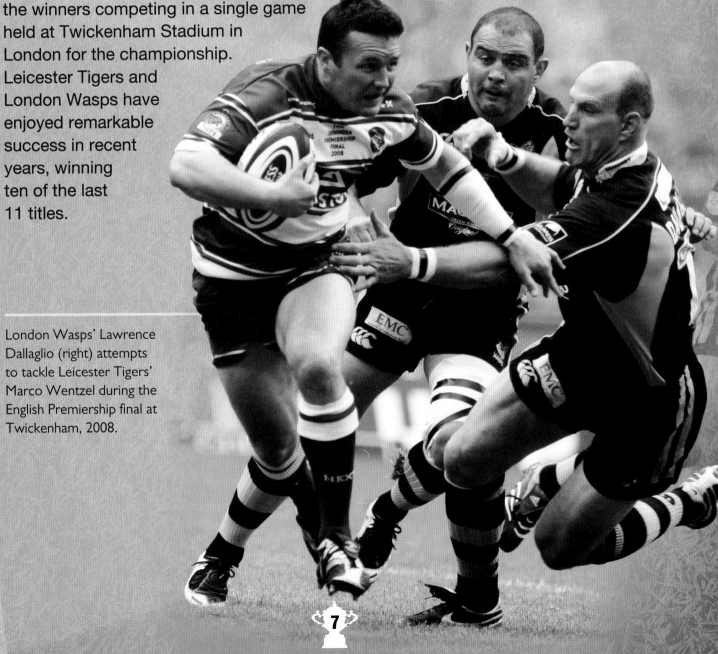

Club rugby league

The two biggest club rugby league competitions in the world are based in Australia (the National Rugby League; Est. 1998) and England (the Super League; Est. 1996). Both end with a single game for the championship, called a Grand Final.

National Rugby League (NRL)

Sixteen teams take part in the National Rugby League. Most are based in the Australian state of New South Wales, but there are also three clubs from Queensland and one, the Warriors, based in New Zealand. August and September is the most intense part of the NRL season, with the top eight teams taking part in play-offs, aiming to reach the Grand Final. With three NRL titles, the Brisbane Broncos are the competition's most successful side.

Jason Nightingale scores for the St. George Illawarra Dragons against the Sydney Roosters in the 2010 NRL Grand Final. The Dragons won 32–8.

The Super League

The 14 Super League teams are mostly from northern England, but also include the Catalan Dragons from France and the Celtic Crusaders from Wales. They play 27 games – 13 home games, 13 away games and a Magic Weekend game where all the teams play a match at a neutral venue. In 2009 and 2010, the Magic Weekend took place at the Murrayfield Stadium in Edinburgh.

The Grand Final

The eight leading Super League teams go into a play-off series of games with the top two taking part in the Grand Final. This is held in October at Manchester United FC's Old Trafford stadium, attracting a crowd of over 60,000. St Helens, the Bradford Bulls and the Leeds Rhinos have reached the Grand Final more often than any other clubs.

World Club Challenge

The winners of the Super League and the NRL champions clash in a single one-off game every year called the World Club Challenge. Recent matches have been dramatic and exciting, such as Super League's St. Helens beating the Brisbane Broncos 18–14 in 2007 or the Leeds Rhinos losing 10–18 to NRL's Melbourne Storm in 2010.

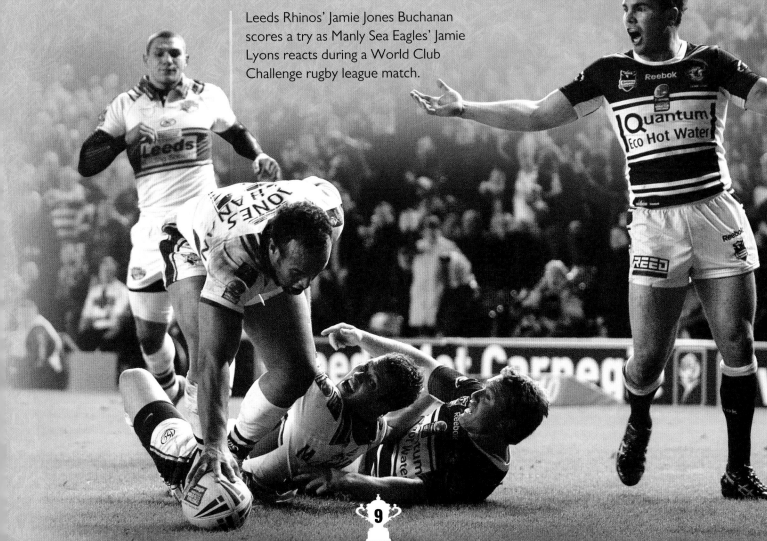

Leeds Rhinos' Jamie Jones Buchanan scores a try as Manly Sea Eagles' Jamie Lyons reacts during a World Club Challenge rugby league match.

The Heineken Cup

The Heineken Cup was formed in 1995 to offer top rugby union clubs in Europe the chance to compete against each other. Teams from England, France, Ireland, Italy, Scotland and Wales, all take part.

Qualification and pools

Teams get to play in the Heineken Cup by finishing in the top positions of their country's league the season before. The tournament begins in October with 24 teams, divided into six groups called **pools**, with the pool winners and two best performing runners-up reaching the tournament's **quarter-finals**.

Making the final

The tension mounts as the tournament reaches the semi-finals and final stages. The Leicester Tigers have reached the final five times, but have only won the Cup twice. Toulouse are the most successful side in the competition, with four titles to their name. They also recorded the Cup's biggest ever win, a 108–16 point thrashing of the Welsh team Ebbw Vale in 1998.

Cardiff Blues' Tom James is tackled by Toulouse's Thierry Dusautoir (left) and Jean Bouilhou during a Heineken Cup quarter-final match in Cardiff.

Marvellous Munster

The Irish team Munster twice reached the Heineken Cup final and lost, before winning the competition in both 2006 and 2008. One of their players, John Hayes, also holds the record for playing in the most Heineken Cup games – 97 in total. In 2009, Munster lost their semi-final to eventual winners, Leinster, but the 82,208 spectators set a world record for a club rugby union game.

European Challenge Cup

Top teams who do not qualify for the Heineken Cup can take part in the European Challenge Cup. It features 20 teams drawn not only from the British, Irish and French leagues, but also four clubs from Italy, one from Spain and Bucureşti Oaks, a Romanian team formed especially to play in this tournament.

The Heineken Cup's leading points scorer, Ronan O'Gara, strikes a penalty for Munster from close to the **touchline.**

GREAT SPORTING STATS

Leading points scorers in the Heineken Cup (1995–2009)

Ronan O'Gara, Ireland: 1,138
Stephen Jones, Wales: 801
Diego Dominguez, Italy: 645
David Humphreys, Ireland: 564
Neil Jenkins, Wales: 502
Dimitri Yachvili, France: 517

Super 14 And Tri-Nations

The leading rugby union-playing nations in the southern hemisphere are Australia, New Zealand and South Africa. They compete as national teams in the Tri-Nations competition, whilst their top club sides take part in a Super 14 competition, which became Super 15 in 2011.

Super 15 scoring

The Super 15 teams play each other once in a season with four points awarded for a win, two for a draw and a **bonus point** for teams scoring more than three tries in a game. The losing team also wins a bonus point if they lose by less than eight points. The top four teams from these matches play in semi-finals.

Competition stars

The Canterbury Crusaders from New Zealand have been the most successful team in the Super 14, as champions seven times and runners-up twice. They hold the record for the biggest win (96–19 against the Waratahs) in 2002, and in 2005 scored the most points in a season (541, including 71 tries).

Andries Bekker of the South African Stormers gains **possession** of the ball during a Super 14 game against the New Zealand Blues in Cape Town, South Africa.

The Tri-Nations

Starting life in 1996, the Tri-Nations pitches Australia, New Zealand and South Africa into a **round robin** tournament. In 2006, the number of games in the Tri-Nations series increased, with each side playing their opponents three times. New Zealand have enjoyed the most success in the competition, winning ten championships, but games can be close. In the last three matches of the 2009 Tri-Nations, Australia beat South Africa who then beat New Zealand who, themselves, then beat Australia. In 2012, Argentina are expected to join the competition to turn it into the Four Nations.

Tri Nations Recent Winners	
2002	New Zealand
2003	New Zealand
2004	South Africa
2005	New Zealand
2006	New Zealand
2007	New Zealand
2008	New Zealand
2009	South Africa
2010	New Zealand

South Africa's John Smit (right) and Victor Matfield lift the 2009 Tri-Nations trophy (left). By beating New Zealand in the final, South Africa also won the Freedom Cup (right).

The Six Nations

In 1883, an international rugby union competition for the **home nations** of the United Kingdom was first held. France who joined in 1910, turned the competition into the Five Nations, which in 2000 became the Six Nations with the arrival of Italy.

Tournament timings

The tournament begins in February with the first round of games and ends in late March. Since 2002, a Six Nations for the same countries' women's teams (except when Spain replaced Italy between 2002 and 2007) has been held at the same time of the year.

Home and away

The Six Nations is a round robin league competition. Teams play five games in total each season. Two or three are at home and the remainder away. At home, the team plays its games in the same stadium each year. Despite three of the stadia holding over 80,000 fans (London's Twickenham, Paris's Stade de France and Ireland's Croke Park), demand for tickets is almost as fierce as some of the play on the pitch.

Ireland play Scotland in the 2006 Six Nations tournament. The Irish won the game 15–9 in the last game at the famous Lansdowne Road stadium before it was redeveloped.

Epic rivalries

Scoring is simple, with two points for a win and one for a draw, but the strong, historic rivalries between teams such as England and Scotland mean that matches are often packed with drama and incident. These include Ireland's narrow 14–13 defeat of England in 2009 and Scotland's last-minute 23–20 win over Ireland in 2010.

Grand Slams

The dream of any team entering the Six Nations is to complete a Grand Slam: winning all five games and the championship as a result. In 2009, Ireland achieved this for the first time since 1948. Back-to-back grand slams have occurred just five times, the last in 1997 and 1998 by France.

GREAT SPORTING STATS

Ireland's Brian O'Driscoll, with 22 tries in 50 matches, is the leading try scorer in the past 50 years of the tournament, but it is England's Jonny Wilkinson who leads the points scoring with 529 points after the 2010 competition.

Ireland's Paul O'Connell is tackled by Italy's Gonzalo Garcia during a Six Nations match. O'Connell captained Ireland to a Six Nations victory in 2009.

Tours and Tests

The rugby world is split between the northern and southern hemispheres, with competitions held at different times of the year. National teams from each hemisphere fly across the planet each year to go on short tours of rival nations.

Summer tours

After the club rugby season has ended in May, British and European national teams often go on tour in early summer. Common destinations are South America to play Argentina and Uruguay, or a daunting visit to the rugby powerhouses of Australia, New Zealand or South Africa which usually takes place in May or June before the Tri-Nations (see page 13) begins.

Dwayne Peel and Ryan Jones, from Wales, take on Jaco van der Westhuyzen, of South Africa, in an international tour match.

Autumn internationals

In October and November most years, the big three southern hemisphere teams, along with teams such as Canada and, sometimes, a Pacific Islanders' side from Fiji, Tonga and Samoa, all tour Europe. They play one or more matches against clubs or regional teams to warm up for big one-off matches against national sides.

Georgia's Giorgi Rokhvadze passes the ball out of the scrum in a match against the USA, during the Churchill Cup.

Tough test

For the host nations of Britain, Ireland and France, the autumn internationals are a tough test. In 2010, for example, Wales faced Australia, South Africa, Fiji and New Zealand in successive weekends. Victories can be rare but notable for the home teams, such as Scotland's defeat of Australia, or Ireland beating the world champions, South Africa, both in 2009.

The Churchill Cup

The Churchill Cup was set up in 2003 and is held in June every year in Canada and North America. It is designed to raise the profile of rugby union in these countries. Their first teams take on second level or younger player sides, such as Ireland A and the England Saxons, from more established rugby-playing countries. The England Saxons won the tournament in 2010.

GREAT SPORTING STATS

In 2009, Scotland's narrow 9–8 win in the autumn international against Australia was their first victory over Australia in over 25 years. The following week, though, Scotland lost 6–9 to another touring team, Argentina.

The British and Irish Lions

The British and Irish Lions is the most famous rugby touring side of all. Players and coaches take on the challenge of a trip once every four years to one of the three biggest rugby-playing nations in the southern hemisphere.

Picking the team

The first tour made by an official Lions team was to South Africa in 1910, although a combined Irish and British team had visited Australia in 1888. Today, a selection panel sits with the head coach and picks players from Ireland, England, Scotland and Wales to form a squad of around 40 players. To be picked to go on a Lions tour is a major honour.

On tour

The Lions have just a few short weeks to train together and get to know their new team-mates before they go on tour. The tour consists of a number of matches against regional teams, and three test matches against the home side's national team, which in 2009 was the world champion, South Africa.

British Lions' scrum-half Dicky Jeeps looks to make a pass during the third Test of the 1955 Lions tour of South Africa.

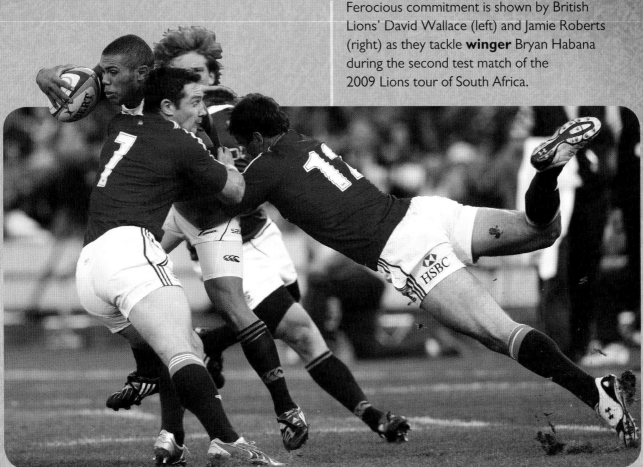

Ferocious commitment is shown by British Lions' David Wallace (left) and Jamie Roberts (right) as they tackle **winger** Bryan Habana during the second test match of the 2009 Lions tour of South Africa.

Dirt trackers

As the tour progresses, many of the players learn that they will not be selected for the first Test. These '**dirt trackers**' will still have to perform in the regional games and support their team-mates, but may get a chance later in the tour. In 2009, Welsh player Shane Williams wasn't selected for the first two Tests, but when he appeared in the third, he scored two tries.

Future secured

Doubts existed over the Lions' future after a 2–1 defeat against Australia in 2001 and a disastrous 3–0 series loss in New Zealand in 2005. These were erased by an incredibly exciting series against South Africa in 2009, where the Lions lost narrowly 2–1, but beat South Africa in the final Test in thrilling style, 28–9. The next Lions tour will take place in Australia in 2013.

GREAT SPORTING STATS

Ireland's Willie John McBride has played the most Tests for the Lions – 17 in total. The three leading Lions pointscorers have all played six Tests – England's Jonny Wilkinson (67 points), Scotland's Gavin Hastings (66 points) and Wales's Stephen Jones (53 points).

International rugby sevens

Rugby sevens is an exciting, attacking version of rugby union played on a full-sized pitch, but with just seven players a side. Games are short and incredibly direct with three-man **scrums** and the emphasis on attacking play.

Points scoring

Tries, penalties and conversions are worth the same in sevens as they are in regular rugby union, although conversions have to be taken as a **drop kick**. Despite games only lasting 14 minutes, with one minute break between halves, scoring can be high. In a 2010 Hong Kong Sevens semi-final, New Zealand beat Fiji 33–28.

One of the greatest ever rugby sevens' players, Fiji's Waisale Serevi, runs for a last try against New Zealand in the Hong Kong Sevens.

Hong Kong Sevens

Teams usually play a series of games in a day or weekend tournament. Amongst the most famous of all tournaments is the Hong Kong Sevens, held at the end of March every year since 1976. There's a festive atmosphere in the crowd and outrageous attacking play on the pitch. This often comes from Pacific island teams such as Fiji who have won the tournament 12 times, including 2009, and Samoa who won it in 2010.

IRB Sevens World Series

This is a series of tournaments run by the International Rugby Board (IRB). The higher a team finishes at a tournament, the more points it earns. The team with the most points in a series is the winner. Samoa won the series in 2010 whilst New Zealand won six times in a row (2000–2006).

Rugby Sevens World Cup

Held every four years (since 1993 for men and 2009 for women), this is the ultimate sevens tournament. England, New Zealand, Fiji and Australia have all won the men's World Cup, whilst Wales became surprise champions in 2009. In the same year, Australia won the first women's tournament.

New Zealand's Zar Lawrence (right) passes the ball while being tackled by Wales's Lee Williams during the semi-finals of the Rugby World Cup Sevens in Dubai, UAE in 2009.

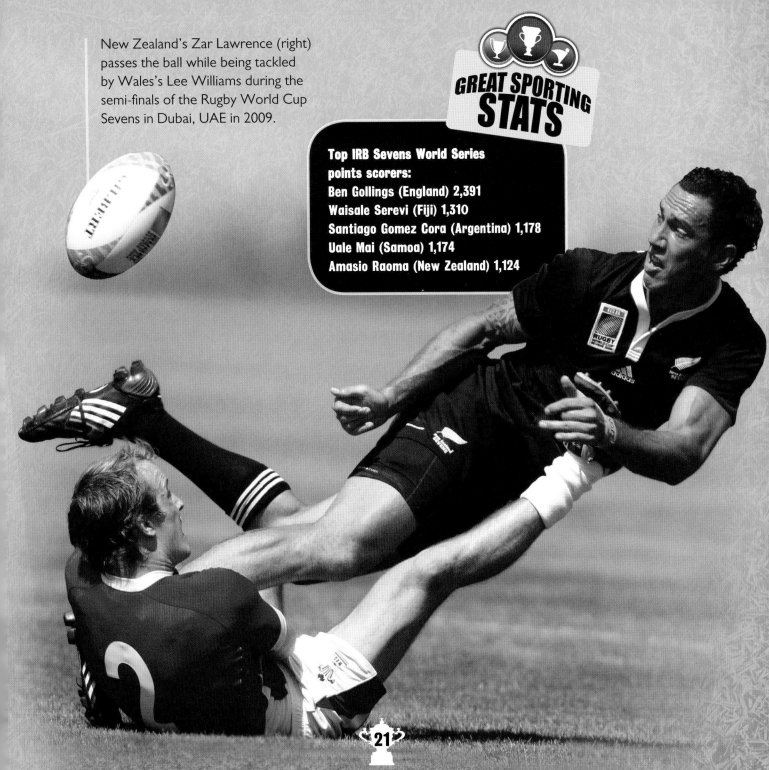

GREAT SPORTING STATS

Top IRB Sevens World Series points scorers:
Ben Gollings (England) 2,391
Waisale Serevi (Fiji) 1,310
Santiago Gomez Cora (Argentina) 1,178
Uale Mai (Samoa) 1,174
Amasio Raoma (New Zealand) 1,124

International rugby league

The Rugby League World Cup was first held in 1954 and is much older than the rugby union version (see pages 24–25). Over the years, the format has changed, but only three teams – Australia, Great Britain and New Zealand – have ever won it.

Expanding numbers

In 1995, the tournament was expanded from five to ten teams, allowing sides such as Samoa, Fiji, South Africa and Tonga to enter for the first time. Team numbers grew to 16 in 2000 with Lebanon and Russia amongst those who joined, but dropped back to ten teams for the next competition, which was held in 2008.

New Zealand's Sam Perrett clashes with Australia's Cameron Smith (right) during the Rugby League World Cup Final in Brisbane, Australia, 2008.

Fabulous finals

Amongst the greatest finals were Australia's nail-biting 13–12 win over Great Britain in 1977, and the 2008 final in which firm favourites, Australia, were beaten 34–20 by New Zealand. Both team captains, Australia's Darren Lockyer and New Zealand's Nathan Cayless, were the only remaining players from the previous World Cup Final back in 2000.

League Tri-Nations

A desire for more regular international rugby league saw the Tri-Nations series between Australia, Great Britain and New Zealand kick off in 1999. The teams played each other once (from 2004, twice) and then the top two teams played a final. Australia and New Zealand both won the competition on two occasions.

In 2009, the competition was replaced by a Four Nations series. The additional team is either the winner of the European Cup (competed for by the top European teams, excluding England) or the Pacific Cup, which in 2010 was Papua New Guinea.

England's Kyle Eastmond is halted by New Zealand's Issac Luke (right) and Kieran Foran (left) during a Four Nations rugby league match.

The Rugby World Cup

The IRB Rugby Union World Cup began in 1987 and is held every four years. From the 100 teams who attempt to qualify, just 20 take part in the tournament. All are hoping to get their hands on the famous Webb Ellis trophy.

The opening match of the 1999 Rugby World Cup between Wales and Argentina kicks off at the Millennium Stadium in Cardiff, Wales. Wales won a hard-fought encounter 23–18.

Hosting nations

World Cup hosts are selected many years ahead to give the countries time to upgrade their facilities. For the 1999 World Cup, for example, Wales built the magnificent Millennium Stadium in Cardiff. Some tournaments are co-hosted, such as in 2007, when France were the main hosts but some games were held in Scotland and Wales. Future tournaments will be held in England in 2015 and Japan four years later.

Massive interest

Only 17,768 people turned up to watch France beat Australia in a pulsating semi-final at the first World Cup. Since that time, the tournament has boomed in popularity. Over 2.2 million people went to see the 48 games played at the 2007 tournament in France, with 80,430 spectators watching the final.

Southern dominance

All the World Cups so far have been won by South Africa, New Zealand or Australia, with the exception of England's 2003 victory, thanks to Jonny's Wilkinson's last-minute drop goal. Many other sides have had their moments of glory, however. At the 2007 tournament Georgia nearly beat a strong Ireland side and Japan narrowly lost to Fiji, who won a thrilling encounter with Wales 38–34. However, the biggest story of the tournament, which was won by South Africa, was Argentina coming third, beating Ireland, Scotland and France twice along the way.

England's Jonny Wilkinson converts another penalty during the Rugby World Cup semi-final against France in 2003.

GREAT SPORTING STATS

Jonny Wilkinson's 243 points for England in three World Cups are the most scored by a player, whilst New Zealand's Grant Fox scored the most in one World Cup with 126 points in 1987. The record try scorer is New Zealand's Jonah Lomu with 15 tries.

Women's rugby

Women's rugby union and rugby league is booming. Teams play under the same rules and on the same size pitches as men, in a variety of competitions for club teams and national sides.

Club rugby league

Australia, New Zealand and England are home to most of the world's women's rugby league clubs. In Australia, competitions are mostly run at state level. The best players from the Australian states of Queensland and New South Wales play each other in matches called State of Origin. In England, 16 teams compete in the women's Rugby League Conference in three divisions. The competition began in 2008 with the 2010 champions being Keighley Cats.

International Rugby League

Four nations – Australia, New Zealand, England and France – compete in rugby league test matches against each other. In 2008, these nations were joined by teams from Tonga, Russia, Samoa and the Pacific Islands to form an eight-team Women's Rugby League World Cup. New Zealand won the competition, beating Australia 34–0 in the final. This tournament is now held once every four years.

New Zealand Maori player, Kellie Kiwi, passes the ball during a Woman's Rugby League World Cup Final.

Club rugby union

Increasingly large numbers of women's rugby union clubs take part in leading cup and league competitions, such as the National Women's Championship in Australia, the Women's All Ireland League and the SWRU Premier League in Scotland. In England, the leading women's teams such as Bristol and Richmond compete in a Premiership league. Below this there are north and south championship leagues.

Women's Rugby Union World Cup

First held in 1991, when the winners were the USA, this competition features 12 teams from all over the world. The 2010 tournament in England included teams from Sweden, Canada and Kazakhstan, as well as South Africa, Australia, Scotland and England. New Zealand won the tournament for the fourth time in a row.

GREAT SPORTING STATS

Carla Hohepa of New Zealand and Canada's Heather Moyse were leading try scorers at the 2010 Women's Rugby Union World Cup with seven tries each. New Zealand were the highest scoring team with 186 points in total.

The New Zealand women's rugby union team celebrate winning the 2010 Rugby World Cup. They beat England 13–10 in a tense final.

WOMEN'S RUGBY WORLD CUP 2010
WINNERS

iRB WOMEN'S RUGBY WORLD CUP 2010

Timeline and winner tables

1871 The first international rugby match between teams from Scotland and England.

1877 A rule change cuts down the number of players in a team from 20 to 15.

1886 The International Rugby Board (IRB) is formed, to run world rugby.

1895 A breakaway group of rugby clubs form the Northern Rugby League.

1896 The first Rugby League Challenge Cup is held.

1910 France joins the Home Nations to form the Five Nations competition.

1924 The last appearance of rugby union at the Olympics.

1954 The Rugby League World Cup is formed.

1971 The number of points for a rugby union try increases from three to four.

1976 The Hong Kong Sevens competition is held for the first time.

1980 The first State of Origin match occurs, between Queensland and New South Wales.

1982 The first official women's international rugby union match, between the Netherlands and France.

1983 The number of points for a rugby league try increases from three to four.

1987 The New Zealand All Blacks win the Rugby World Cup, beating France in the final.

1991 The first Women's Rugby Union World Cup is hosted in Wales.

1992 The number of points for a rugby union try increases from four to five points.

1993 The first Rugby Sevens World Cup, is held at Murrayfield, in Edinburgh.

1995 IRB declares rugby union to be an open sport, allowing full professionalism for the first time.

1996 The Tri-Nations Rugby Union series starts between Australia, New Zealand and South Africa.

1996 Rugby League's Super League begins.

1998 The National Rugby League competition starts in Australia.

2000 The Five Nations becomes the Six Nations when Italy joins.

2003 England win their first ever Rugby Union World Cup, beating Australia.

2011 The Rugby Union World Cup in New Zealand.

2016 First Olympics to include rugby sevens as a medal sport.

The British Lions play South Africa during their four-match series in 1955.

28

Winner tables

Men's Rugby Union World Cup

Year	Winners	Runners-up
1987	New Zealand	France
1991	Australia	England
1995	South Africa	New Zealand
1999	Australia	France
2003	England	Australia
2007	South Africa	England

Women's Rugby Union World Cup

Year	Winners	Runners-up
1991	USA	England
1994	England	USA
1998	New Zealand	USA
2002	New Zealand	England
2006	New Zealand	England
2010	New Zealand	England

Rugby Sevens World Cup (Men's)

Year	Winners	Runners-up
1993	England	Australia
1997	Fiji	South Africa
2001	New Zealand	Australia
2005	Fiji	New Zealand
2009	Wales	Argentina

Rugby League World Cup (Men's)

Year	Winners	Runners-up
1954	Great Britain	France
1957	Australia	Great Britain
1960	Great Britain	Australia
1968	Australia	France
1970	Australia	Great Britain
1972	Great Britain	Australia
1975	Australia	England
1977	Australia	Great Britain
1985–88	Australia	New Zealand
1989–92	Australia	Great Britain
1995	Australia	England
2000	Australia	New Zealand
2008	New Zealand	Australia

Glossary and further info

Bonus points A system used in some league competitions of awarding extra points to teams for close games or for scoring many tries.

Conversion A kick awarded after a try, which, if it travels between the goal posts, is worth two points.

Dirt trackers A slang term given to players in a touring squad who tend only to play in the less important matches of a tour.

Drop goal A points-scoring move where the ball is kicked out of the hand between the goalposts.

Drop kick A kick made from the hands with the ball dropped down and struck just before it reaches the ground.

Foul A breaking of the rules of a game of rugby such as tackling an opponent in a dangerous manner.

Home nations The countries that make up the United Kingdom: England, Scotland, Wales and Northern Ireland.

Intercepting When a member of the defending team gathers the ball during a pass made by the opposing team.

Lineout A way of restarting play in rugby union when the ball has left the side of the pitch. The ball is thrown into the middle of rows of players from each team.

Pools Small groups of teams in some rugby competitions who all play each other with one or more teams qualifying from the pool to play in the next round of the tournament.

Possession When a player or team has the ball under control.

Quarter-final The four games played with the four winners taking part in the semi-final of a competition.

Round robin A type of competition format where each team plays all the other teams in their group.

Scrum A way of restarting play which involves eight players a side in rugby union and six players per side in rugby league.

Semi-final The two games played with the two winners taking part in the final of a competition.

Tactics Styles of play and moves which a team and a coach work on to try to beat the opposing team.

Touchline The lines marking the side edges of the pitch.

Try Getting the ball placed down under control in the in-goal area of the pitch which is worth five points in rugby union and four in rugby league

Wingers Fast, attacking players in both rugby league and rugby union who have to defend but aim to create or score tries.

Websites

http://www.irb.com
The official website of the International Rugby Board, the organisation that runs international rugby union including the World Cup.

http://www.rugbyworldcup.com
The 2011 Rugby World Cup website with details of qualifying, fixtures and statistics from all the past competitions.

http://www.rbs6nations.com/en/home.php
The official website of the Six Nations competition.

http://www.ercrugby.com/eng/312_11.php
A website about European club rugby with lots of information and news on the Heineken Cup.

http://www.rugby.com.au
The official website of Australian rugby union offers up to the minute coverage of both the Australian national rugby union team, the Tri-Nations and all the Super 14 action.

http://www.super14.com
The official website of the Super 14 contest gives all the details of the current tournament as well as information on previous competitions.

http://www.scrumqueens.com
An information-packed website for women's international rugby union with news of tournaments from all around the world.

http://www.planet-rugby.com
Learn more about international rugby union at this website with news and competitions searchable by country.

http://www.scrum.com
A website packed with news, views, photos, results and statistics on rugby union all over the planet.

http://www.rugbysevens.co.uk
A useful website for newcomers to rugby sevens with rules and playing guides as well as details of leading sevens tournaments in Britain and abroad.

http://www.rleague.com
The World of Rugby League website is a feast of facts, news and profiles from all the main rugby league playing nations.

http://www.therfl.co.uk/index.php
The Rugby Football League website has a handy guide to the game as well as details of all levels of rugby league competition.

Further reading

Rugby – Paul Morgan (A&C Black Publishers Ltd, 2008)
A good starting guide to the sport and its leading players.

Know Your Sport: Rugby – Clive Gifford (Franklin Watts, 2010)
Find out about rugby tactics and techniques and some of the world's biggest tournaments.

Index